MW00413575

COLLISION COURSE

4Fs®™ to Transform Life's Challenges
into Powerful Breakthroughs

Lynn,

Hope you enjoy the book and
thank you for supporting! This
book might display some gems
to reach your next breakthrough.
This is more than a car crash
but a testimony into how I
managed to pour into my purpose.
You are amazing and stay the course!

- Phil
4/7/9

Collision Course. Copyright © 2018 by Phillip Terrill. All rights reserved. Printed in the United States. No part of this book may be reproduced, stored in a retrieval system, or transmitted in any form or by any means, electronic, mechanical, photocopying, recording, or otherwise, without express written permission, except in the case of brief quotations embodied in critical articles and reviews.

Published by Phillip Terrill
1201 Robert Street South, Ste.3-18235
St. Paul, MN 55118
ISBN: 9781543935691
Library of Congress Cataloging-in-Publication Data

Book Cover Design by ebooklaunch.com

Introduction

Collision Course is built on the foundation of the 4F®™ Model—a comprehensive approach to balancing life and breaking through its toughest challenges. Within the pages to follow, buckle up and learn how one moment in time transformed a life forever. *My goal is not just to tell you a story...It is my hope that my personal testimony will provide a life-changing perspective that may help to guide you in the future!*

In the last three years, I have learned about the beauty and fragility of life. Take a moment and reflect on what you have accomplished, where you want to go, and what it will take to achieve your wildest dreams. They are attainable. All you must do is take action.

Get to work, and I'll see you on the other side!

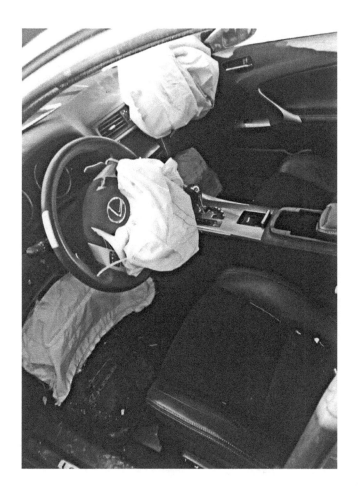

CONTENTS

"Short term sacrifice for long term success."

—Keith James

COLLISION COURSE

DECEMBER 20, 2014
ATLANTA, GEORGIA

1

Wake Up Call
Part 1

It was five days until Christmas, and there I was, enjoying another momentous occasion. In December in Atlanta, the weather was not the typical Minneapolis tundra that I was accustomed to experiencing around that time of the year. There was no snow, and folks were enjoying another Saturday in Georgia. You could tell the holidays were right around the corner, as wreaths lined the neighborhood doors, and a discoverable sense of cheer was present. I remember later that evening talking to some friends about all of us getting together. I do not even recall the occasion, but it was the first time in a while that the fellas had hung out, so we were sure going to have a good time—we always did! Once we got together, I could tell it was going to be a memorable evening. The pre-game ritual was always to tap the bottom of the bottle and pass it around, so everyone could "approve" the libation. Classic hip-hop tunes and top tracks filled the house. With drinks in hand, our epic journey in the "A" was drawing near. It was time to hit the city! The guys grabbed their stylish shoes and blazers for what always seemed to be a semi-fashion show—at least for some of us, looking sharp was a big deal. I was always impressed by how seriously my friends detailed out their wardrobes or took infamous shopping trips to Lenox Mall. It was like they intentionally left their clothes at home just to have an excuse to go there.

We had all met in undergrad at Tuskegee University, so there was a unique brotherhood feel to our kinship. I call it kinship because at that point in our lives, we were no longer friends, we were brothers. As the brothers finished strapping up their monk strap dress shoes, (or for some, their designer sneakers) we loaded up in what seemed to be a caravan, or parade of nice automobiles. I remember the feeling of pride when I pressed my foot on the brake and tapped the start button of my car at the time. The car was a gift from my mother and stepfather for graduating as an undergrad on time. There is a funny story behind my mention of "on time," and a close friend knows exactly what I mean. The roar of my Lexus F Sport was thunderous. The LED lighting in the car illuminated everything perfectly.

The level of detail was obvious, from the stitching on the steering wheel to the bass in the speakers. A car can definitely be a reflection of its owner, and in this case, that was true.

As we arrived at our initial destination, the guys were having a great time, and the evening was flowing smoothly. Each night out together was a celebration of success, a toast to our triumphs, an acknowledgement of our failures, and a platform to praise each other as brothers. Somehow, we built this trust and sacred space amongst ourselves that allowed us to enjoy each other for exactly who, and where we were. I recall looking around that night and reflecting on how lucky a guy must be to have seven or eight friends that he can depend on like brothers every day. There was a fearlessness to how we approached our lives, and we continue to do so. I am incredibly thankful for the circle!

As we kicked it and let our Saturday evening continue, the drinks flowed faster, and the checks kept coming. From spot to spot, we made moves a GPS couldn't keep up with. The last place we ended up was Decatur, Georgia, near my best friend's house. We had been to this particular lounge a few times, knowing it was an excellent place to meet new folks, dance a little, and have some fine drinks. By that time, it was around 2:00 a.m. The city was shutting down, and it was time to make our way home. There is something about alcohol that makes a person feel invincible. Fear is nonexistent, and life becomes unbreakable. I learned a long time ago from my mother that "nothing good happens past midnight," and that night was going to knock that axiom right out of the ballpark. Her words would be made crystal clear, and then further emphasized by God. Historically, my family has a recognizable ability to deflect pain, confusion, angst, or anything that resembles weakness. Whether it's sports, shopping, religion, or even alcohol, every one of us has our vice(s), making facing our demons difficult, and any effort to stop is equivalent to trying to move a mountain, or impede a locomotive without brakes.

When we were traveling home after our night of partying, I could feel the strong buzz commonly associated with drinking too much. I did what most young adults would do, despite having access to modern-day services like Uber. My "macho" or "invincibility" complex had me sitting behind the wheel of what was essentially that locomotive without brakes. Speeding down the street, trying to make a sharp left turn, and jumping over the median, I knocked down a tree. Suddenly, there I was, sitting in the middle of oncoming traffic with a totaled vehicle. My heart pounded, and my concern immediately gravitated towards my friends. "Are you ok? Are you alright? Hurt?" I uttered to my friends, my boys, the fellas. There were three of us in the car—Jeremy, Corey, and me. I can remember the anxiety I felt as I sat behind the wheel, trying to force the vehicle to accelerate from its crushed position. The damage had occurred, and there was no going back.

I realized in that instant that I was no longer Superman, or even an ounce close to that persona. I was a young kid so afraid of the consequences that I forced myself to mull over what would happen next. *What should I do about this?* My car was totaled, my friends were okay, and the road ahead was unclear. Other drivers were passing by, slowly asking if we were all right, or getting out to assess our potential injuries. The ensuing hours were dreadful. The sobriety test that I failed proved to be another moment of confused confidence. I thought my athletic abilities would pull me through when I was asked to stand on one leg or walk in a straight line with one foot in front of the other. I was no longer the same person. I was afraid and insecure about the decisions I had made that evening. I questioned my "brothers" for allowing me to sit behind the wheel. Or was it the fault of the various lounges for somehow letting me buy too many of those Old Fashioneds everyone knows I love? Nonetheless, I was especially intimidated and fearful of phoning my parents to say that I had totaled a vehicle, was intoxicated, and was now in the DeKalb County Prison.

I can recall the entire process as if it were yesterday, and it still pains me to think of making that call. My mother was so prideful, and my stepdad believed in my maturity. All of that was lost as their youngest child and member of the family business made the significantly detrimental decision to drive drunk. Typically, I consider myself to be extremely responsible, and beyond thoughtful about how I conduct myself in public. No matter what I believed about myself before, I started to reflect on why this happened to me. I would constantly ask God, why did he do *this* to me? What was the purpose, given what I was hoping to accomplish in my life? God knew my prayers and my heart. So, why would He take that from me in an instant? The answer was elusive until a few months later, but it eventually became clear to me that it was all for a great reason.

I began to realize that God wanted me to learn a new lesson. He sought to break me down to remove the many personas I had created against His will. God wanted me to stop hiding from who He wanted me to become. By shedding my immaturity and weakness, I could become so much more. This process of being broken created many more peaks and valleys to my new journey. He put me on a path to self-discovery, so I could learn who I was and not who I let society make me. God restored my self-control; that is powerful! Think about what God wants you to become and who He wants you to be. This will create numerous pathways and deliver a vivid vision. If you let Him willingly guide your steps, you will experience a rebirth. The evolution of a person does not always begin with a traumatic experience; it can just come from wanting to experience change. But you need to be open to experiencing a different version of yourself that can impact the world more positively than you ever thought before. A version that only you know to be right and true. Take the time to invest in yourself today, so who you are tomorrow is the best you. Take a lesson from my mistake and harness each opportunity to make room for yourself. That space is extremely important as you continue to find your purpose. After the accident, I knew that in due-time this evolution would happen, and it would be just what I needed to reach my breakthrough.

"Develop an odor of success! When people smell you, they know the steps to take to become who they want to be."

—Corey Williams

COLLISION COURSE

December 21, 2014
Atlanta, Georgia

2

Wake Up Call
Part 2

This book is not about me being politically correct; neither is it about my professional career, or the opinions of society. It is a way to finally say, "This is who I am, and I made a mistake." *Collision Course* aims to encourage young people to step up and be responsible, so that they can enjoy the abundance of life. Think critically about your actions and decisions. Everything we do in our lives impacts some other person, and I vowed to myself that I would never have to make a call like that to my mother again. The road to redemption is tough, grueling, embarrassing, confusing, and exhausting, but what happens when you reach that breakthrough is what *Collision Course* is all about. Run full force into the old you—that challenge, or your problems—and say, "Today will be different. I am focused on change and will regain control." What you can accomplish when you're in control is incredible. The life you seek and the challenges you constantly face are no longer massive tribulations that seem insurmountable. Those challenges become avoidable, and agility can be restored into our movements.

The flow of life is elevated, and even small victories taste sweet.

During this process, I developed a model for approaching each step of the accident, and my life after that. This simple methodology would lend consistency and organization to how I navigate my life. I learned early on that a strong foundation is the key to being successful. I needed to revisit my roots as a kid—roots that were planted in education, and self-reflection. I considered what I wanted this model to represent as I opened myself to this world of emotions after the crash. Indeed, it was quite simple: I wanted to be able to compartmentalize every step into four areas of my natural behavior. These areas include Find, Focus, Feed, and Facts, which I will delve into more deeply later, but I wanted to give you an idea of the structure of the model.

Naturally, one would ask: *from where did this model originate?* Let me give you some background on what I call the *4F®™ Model* for turning life's challenges into powerful breakthroughs. What is the 4F®™ Model? How do you effectively break

what of course I've been missing since childhood

down and solve problems to drive results? People approach every moment in life by analyzing the benefits and repercussions of their actions based on instinctive measurement. This is an intuitive and internal process dictated by our logic, our experiences, our intellect, and sometimes our "gut." I have developed and implemented the 4F®™ Model for the last four years, but now it is time to share it with others. The 4F®™ Model focuses on developing strategies and processes, unique to your desired outcomes or dreams, to navigate the marathon of life's opportunities. It helps you tackle those moments and identify successful tactics to grow beyond your current environment, and continuously add value to your journey.

As you read through this playbook and apply the model to your daily life, think about what you can do to expand each area of your life for greater success. You achieve the most exceptional outcomes by being flexible, and by investing a ridiculous amount of energy into those desired results. My life experiences will be illustrated in a very

Apply to daily life !

Are we focusing on increasing success, or surviving + thriving in adversity?

transparent manner that reflects my victories, lessons learned from defeat, and triumphs over challenges by leveraging the 4F®™ Model. *Collison Course* is about how one evening in December changed my life and sparked the resurgence of a life delivered through the will of God.

On this journey, I realized that each area may not be prevalent in every scenario, but I find myself evaluating situations at all four levels. This kind of self-reflection has helped elevate my thinking and in fact, all facets of my life. The journey of life—and one's ability to respond to its shifting challenges—sometimes makes it difficult to ask the right questions to get the correct answers. We naturally delay our attention and redirect our energy towards other things to minimize the hard work needed to truly identify what it is we are subconciously seeking. That is the exact purpose of this book—helping you unlock the tools to harness your energy and find out what you truly desire for your relationships, your career, and your personal life. To genuinely and objectively identify what those desires are, you must take the

[handwritten margin note: levels — not all necessary]

first step of t[...]
are seeking. [...]
and why? Wh[...]
What are you[...]

As I was [...]
understand ar[...]
and the lives o[...]
hend how the[...]
I discovered t[...]
influencers, le[...]

COLLISION C[...]

challenge the status o[...]
that push the bo[...]
that constant [...]
unique opp[...]
and co[...]
what[...]

a relentless journey to find something or solve a problem. They had an unquenchable thirst and enduring appetite for success, and once they identified that "FIND," they were able to take a step back and start to construct a plan of action. We will discuss that later in the book.

This plan must consist of both tactical and strategic elements that everyone innately possesses. We develop these elements or success traits as soon as we are born. Organically, people are curious, intelligent, and focused on driving tremendous results that make a direct impact. This curiosity demands that we continuously

uo with ingenuity and ideas
ndaries of the ordinary. From
pushing of boundaries comes the
ortunity to experience new moments,
tinuously challenge ourselves to FIND
we so desperately seek.

Within that journey, however, we often hit roadblocks or obstacles that appear insurmountable, but that is when our hunger and resiliency arise, allowing us to push forward. *The fear of problems or obstacles drives us to find success and overcome those challenges.* Conquering those obstacles and removing these roadblocks makes it easier to appreciate and understand the FIND so much better. You are able to enjoy your discovery even more because now you have identified problems, overcome challenges, and gained clarity as to which direction to go, and how to proceed. Remember that curiosity drives discovery, discovery creates experience, and experience inspires change. That new change creates a dynamic catalyst propelling you to the next breakthrough. Step through that opening to your next opportunity.

In creating the 4F®™ Model and this book, I had to question my desires, and identify what I was trying to find. One moment in my life—when I discovered the beauty of just being able to live— influenced my journey immensely, and led me to understand and evaluate my abilities, wishes, hopes, and dreams. I experienced a traumatic moment of vulnerability and weakness at a very young age, and it gave me a unique perspective on the talents I possessed that could spark greatness in myself and make an impact out in the world. But how could I begin to visualize what I yearned to find? For me, the answer was simple: Pray!

My spiritual journey has been incredible. Everyone experiences powerful and titanic moments in their life that shift their perspective of existence and illuminate the path for which they can order their steps (or have them ordered for them). That is the beautiful thing about spirituality, and whatever or whomever you believe in. You can always get a better answer and direction to go towards, if you're willing to ask for it. That moment of clarity was terrific in directing my ability to precisely apply the 4F®™ model to my life in every circumstance. Ultimately, that fostered the critical thinking that allows me to compartmentalize and separate the opportunity into these four steps, which holistically, address any situation. As you approach an opportunity, ask yourself what you are trying to FIND. Write down the ASK and start to support that question with reasons why you are trying to accomplish that. What do you need to get there? Only then can you view the larger picture with a greater sense of purpose and direction. *Example: If you are seeking to be in a successful relationship, ask yourself what you are trying to FIND with or within that other person. Then, support that with notions around why you want those qualities, and what other characteristics or elements that person should possess in order to align with your plan.* Once you have spent enough time with that person and believe that you are making a positive decision, you then begin to move into stage two of the 4F®™ Model: Focus.

The first "F" is the most critical element in adequately executing the remaining steps of the model. If you can properly and authentically ask yourself why and know exactly what you are seeking, finding the answers will be a great deal easier. Authenticity is key in identifying what you are looking for because often, we (people) are very much consumed by societal perceptions or constraints that paralyze our ability to make decisions. We lose sight of who we are, what we are capable of, and what we want to do. The 4F®™ Model in *Collision Course* helps you avoid or remove that paralysis and see the opportunities that await you. God has delivered you time and time again, so why would He stop now? Consider yourself His most precious creation at all times. Stop worrying about the haters and claim what He has built specifically for you. Just because we have a collision doesn't mean we must go off course. Keep moving!

"Find your tribe. The ones that challenge you daily, inspire you wholeheartedly and pray for you unasked. Find them and stick with them."

—John Bailey

COLLISION COURSE

DECEMBER 22, 2014
ATLANTA, GEORGIA

3

Deferred Dreams

Following such a traumatic experience, I remember seeking solitude, as well as some place where I might find answers to the many questions I had after the accident. My family was devastated by my terrible decision to drink and drive. However, I believe it was the process of potentially losing my life that was the most concerning. The hours spent at the DeKalb County Jail were embarrassing. It wasn't until after they processed me into the system and took my mug shot that I felt a pure disgust for myself that I never thought I would know. The smell of justice had a stench I couldn't forget, as people shuffled in and out of the large holding cell—a cell filled with young men facing everything from hard time, to petty misdemeanors. It's amazing how you grow up trying to avoid experiencing life from this perspective, but it was when I sat in the holding cell and talked to other guys that I learned I could still be great, it just would have to be accomplished a bit differently than I anticipated.

As time passed, I found myself processing my next moves, and the impact that night would have on the rest of my life. I wanted to right the wrong and turn back the hands of time so that I could choose to take an Uber or Lyft ride home, but that was not my reality. There I was, in jail for driving under the influence, and wrecking a gift from my parents. How ungrateful could I have been to do such a thing? No matter how many times I tried to convince myself that this nightmare would end, it was just beginning. After sitting in jail for a while and then posting bond, I realized that I would have to face the harsh reality of confronting my parents. I remember getting to their house and anticipating the wrath that any parent would unleash on their child. This was a major thing! I didn't have a simple fender bender or run a light. I had totaled a vehicle while drunk!

My saving grace might have been that it was the holidays. The family was in town and we were all preparing to spend time over at my aunt's house not too far away. The reverberations of my accident traveled like wildfire to everyone in the family. So, attending family events over the holidays was not all laughter and smiles, but a rude awakening that what I had been working hard to build and pursue was crumbling right before my eyes. I knew the impact of my actions was tremendous, and the path to redemption would be tough. This is where I want to share some valuable insight. No matter what you are facing, move forward, and do not let anything stop your progress. I realized that my actions created many adverse outcomes, but it didn't determine what I would become, and how I would accept my responsibilities. I realized that sometimes our dreams become deferred. We must grind and push harder than ever to achieve our goals and make those dreams our realities. This delay was timely, and God knew exactly what He was doing! He was spotlighting that I had so much to improve on and develop before I could reach my next destination to represent His glory!

Through everything, I learned about the people around me and how impactful this rebuilding process was going to be in my development. We must remain patient, silent, and open-minded to pivot in the process, learning that control is something that we need to maintain, but direction is rooted in faith. At this point, I am sure you must be wondering why this chapter was about "deferred dreams" and the connection to the story. Well, let me illustrate it a bit more for you. When I moved back to Atlanta from Chicago in the summer of 2013, a unique opportunity widened my vision. I had the chance to invest my talents in the company my stepfather had built over the last twenty years. The company was doing well, but I started to envision a lifetime commitment to becoming an entrepreneur and being a small part of contributing to the longevity of a legacy. It was the chance to work and learn from my family.

Of course, with any family business, managing the delicate balance between the personal and professional is exceptionally challenging, especially with personality clashes and constant power struggles. The relentless pursuit of incremental revenue and the pressure of meeting payroll was taxing, to say the least. When things were going well, there was golf and travels. Of course, the reverse was the case during the challenging times. That is the nature of entrepreneurship and running a mid-size company with hundreds of people depending on sound decisions from their leadership. As my accident continued to create new hurdles for me to overcome, the tension within our family grew as well, from the strain of the insurance claim on the business, to the outrageous arguments that would ensue on a constant basis, targeting character versus the value of lives saved.

At the time, it seemed our focus was on business and not the lives that were spared after the accident. I share this intentionally, as I want to assure you that no matter the circumstance, you have to develop or build your armor. People, no matter who they are, will always try to deter you from your destiny—greatness! I had to shelter myself with the love of God to reassure myself of my greatness and protect my future. The dream that I once thought was deferred was somehow waiting in a new package. As you face the challenges in life, never stop chasing or working towards your dreams. Often, these dreams will be masked or disguised in a variety of other ways.

Keep grinding and pushing, because the more you put pressure on a rock, the more likely it will turn into a diamond. You must do the same with your dreams. Apply that pressure and align it with hard work to see what gems reveal themselves to you. I promise it will be worth it!

Looking back, the two years I spent working in that environment in the family business was priceless. I felt that pressure every day to perform at a high level and provide a unique impact on the business. The more time I spent learning, investing, and growing in the company, the more I was able to build skills that I can utilize today! You never know the actual purpose of an experience until you move on to the next one. Stay invested and present in today so that tomorrow will have more value. People often dive into every opportunity but do not flourish because they rushed the previous experience. That experience was created to provide you with skills, perspective, or tools that will prepare you for glory.

As my time at the family business wound up, one thing emerged from the journey. I was mastering a creative craft that could sustain me through a tough period that was on the horizon. Without a traditional income, how would I survive? How would I build and grow? The answer to those questions was straightforward, because I rooted myself in the current experience. I maximized everything I could while in the moment until the time came when I had to see what I was capable of while depending on my abilities alone. Never lose sight of your gifts! God didn't create you to be just like everyone around you. If that were true, we would all look and be the same. Walk your path with purpose and know that persistence over time will always deliver results. No matter the height of the climb, stay focused on the battle to the top. Focus on the moment you can release your acceptance and gratitude after surviving a test. Come out strong and experience the meaning of living.

Dreams were meant to be dreams; we can chase them and never lose sight of the influence they create in our daily pursuits. Keep dreaming and fighting for what you want out of life. This life is not a dress rehearsal, so go harder every day to reach that dream destination. If you don't, the life you dreamed of will become a nightmare because you weren't willing to work relentlessly to pursue God's gift to you! I refuse to let you suffer the feeling I had, knowing that my (tremendously) negative actions would defer the realization of my dream of potentially becoming a leader in the family business. In retrospect, the accident was the best thing that happened in my life. It made me put my life goals into perspective and leverage the 4F®™ Model in real time. We will talk about that more as we continue through the book.

"You can't expect to achieve a million- dollar salary with a minimum wage work ethic."

—Raphael Malbrue

COLLISION COURSE

JANUARY 1, 2015
KANSAS CITY, MISSOURI

4

"Straight" Royal

Many of you are probably imagining what this chapter might be about, and how it fits into the broader message. After the accident, I thought the worst had passed, and that my tribulations were over. I believed my tough times were resolved, and I deserved instant happiness. The reality was remarkably different! Before I tell you this part of the story, let me preface it with some of my learnings. Often, when people face challenges and tribulations, they immediately turn to prayer or spirituality. They hope that somehow through faith, all their immediate and future problems will be absorbed into their conversations with a higher power.

Let me give you a real testimony and insight into how this works. I was only able to understand faith when I focused on myself. I needed to learn who I was (and who I was not), so I could ask for help. I needed to differentiate what I needed, from what I expected from my asking for help. Know who you are and what you need before you ask! The other lesson I learned was that you need to pray *before* you hit a hard time. It is not a one-sided discussion that happens only when you want something to work out or need help for your immediate crisis, dismissing the fact that you didn't speak to God when things were going right. Real strength comes from having that discussion all the time, during the highs and lows. Let's be clear: I have not perfected this practice, nor have I figured out the right formula for immediate results. I don't think that will ever happen, but what I do know is that having that conversation consistently will yield enormous outcomes. Try it and see what kinds of changes happen in your life!

Now, whenever I think of asking for help, I recall the reason I wanted to include this chapter as a crucial component of my broader challenge. This section of my book reveals a tremendously important element of who I am, and what I was destined to become in the future. I learned that in the process of not facing the challenging moments, our problems often get compounded until too much pressure builds up and breaks us. However, if you want to achieve the life you wished for when you were little, you must not worry about how much you can take—what matters is how much you can overcome while still pushing towards your dreams.

Two weeks after my accident, I was reflecting on the challenges ahead when my dad called to give me some news that would change the course of our relationship. There was immediate silence on his end after I answered the phone. My dad, usually a stoic individual, paused for too long on the phone. A familiar, unsettling chill spread through my veins. The message was that my grandfather, Penny, had passed away. He was eighty-nine, and full of the sweetest energy a human could possess. I knew this was tough for my father. At that time, we were working on rebuilding our distant relationship, and the passing of my grandfather might have been the reason we accelerated that healing process.

It is amazing how tragedy or pain brings people together and strengthens their relationships. If you have read this far, learn from my mistake of waiting until my grandfather passed away to honestly consider if you have done enough to show how much you care about the people you love. Small things like calling to check on your grandparents, letting go of grudges, loving harder, or simply offering forgiveness can go such a long way. In this case, I wish that would have worked harder towards that outcome. I wished that I made one last phone call to my grandfather, or watched baseball (his favorite pastime) with him one more time.

Baseball was something that Grandpa "Penny" loved. He would watch the Kansas City Royals play repeatedly, whether it was back-to-back wins, or another long season filled with losses. The team hadn't been good in years, but some recent acquisitions had them off to a magical start to the season. I remember getting more into the Royals that year, since Penny was such a fan. The funny thing about Penny was that I never really saw him in a Royals baseball cap, but I knew he was a lifelong fan. It was amazing to see him sit on his couch in his small apartment on Prospect Avenue, watching his Royals while smoking a cigar. Smells of tobacco filled his place, but the love cut through clear as crystal.

Grandpa Penny was a smooth man, but he was hardworking as well. The experience of a thirty-plus-year career on the railroad gave him a certain presence and made his laid-back demeanor something I wanted to emulate, as it was captivating. He seldom—actually never—referred to me by my name. At least, I cannot recall it, and even if I could, there was something that I liked about the way he was always asking my dad, "Where is that boy? Let me give him some money." For me, that memory will never fade. When I did talk to him, in person or on the phone, I would ask, "How are you, Grandpa Penny?" And without hesitation, he would reply, "I'm straight." Such a perfect line from an incredible man! As the patriarchal figure, he built a strong family full of characters, full of life, and full of love.

When I look back on the impact he made, I can see it wasn't just a financial tidbit here or there. The impact was through my dad, whom he loved hard. That distant, yet direct love made my dad want to love me more. He wanted to love me harder than ever imaginable, and as a young, black man growing up with a single parent, I always felt that. The death of my Grandpa Penny gave new life to my relationship with my dad, and that is a beautiful outcome! The trip to my grandfather's funeral was somber but filled with appreciation. The guns banged the 21-gun salute, paying respect to his service in the United States Navy. It was deafening. The gesture reminded me that my family helped protect our nation, but more so, that my grandfather did that for his family. His service in Pearl Harbor and World War II was amazing!

As I watched my family pay tribute, I sat there reflecting about how I could change, or do what I wanted. People come and go; what matters is how you live. Learning how to manage relationships and rebuild as you climb is equally essential. That is what I had to do and needed to do with my father. I made it a point of duty to not let another second go by without me working on that relationship! As you think about my experience, consider your relationships. Imagine how much more vibrant and rewarding your life would be if you made an effort to change. Sometimes, people will not be ready for what you are expecting, but that shouldn't change how you live. Focus on how you can impact those around you by leading them to a place of communication and clarity—an environment that fosters dialogue, understanding, and positive thinking. The journey to reconciliation and rebirth through loss is hard. God (or whomever) will never give you more to deal with than you can handle!

During this time, I thought it was mere punishment for my previous actions. This was the lower level of hell, but really, it was the rock bottom. Sometimes it feels like hell because it is, and that feeling won't change unless you keep moving forward. Keep going! The destination of reaching your dreams does not change or disappear because times got tougher. Desire that destination, and your mindset should shift into a more powerful gear to accelerate your journey to the positive. Never did I imagine that I would be praying daily about how I could still reach my dreams and goals without being crushed by the pressure of the moment. Instead, I focused on the controllable, and relentlessly strived to make my life better and did everything possible to make it happen. This was a brick-by-brick effort, and not something I did all at once. But I, like you, were built for the long haul, and not meant to do it all at once, so that is okay.

As you seek reconciliation, take your time and get the details right, so those relationships prosper for the long term. Never waste energy investing in a short-term outcome or minimal return. You are worth way too much - **"Straight" Royal!**

"Learn from your past failures, so that your future is full of endless possibilities."

—Archie Clay III

COLLISION COURSE

AUGUST 16, 2015
Fargo, North Dakota

5

The Right Formula

Think back to chapter one, where I introduced the concept of the 4F®™ Model. The first element was discovering the FIND and understanding precisely what you were evaluating. In my case, my accident back in 2014 helped me identify what I was hoping to discover—myself. The time between the accident, my grandfather's passing, and my moving to Fargo, North Dakota was very enlightening. That time provided me with an opportunity to figure out what I wanted to do and to experience humility in real time. I needed to learn that whatever my next move was, it should be the best move in terms of the plan or goals for my life. Keep that in mind every time as you evaluate and determine what to invest yourself in: you have to identify, and consistently live for, and work towards *your* aspirations.

Before the accident, I was so caught up in trying to live out the dreams of others that I almost forgot that it was most important to achieve mine. Beyond that, I needed to attain professional success and personal growth on my terms. As a result,

I did consulting and design work for a while before starting the job-hunting process. Those who haven't had the need or desire to search for a job may not know that it is hard work. I was focused on my next life experience, and that desire propelled my search. I went for a few interviews but wasn't landing on that "right" fit.

However, everything changed in the summer of 2015, when a mentor at the time mentioned an opportunity to work at Microsoft. I had just flown back from interviewing with Google in California. That was indeed a process and an honor to see Mountain View from that perspective. I was intrigued by what tech companies were doing and was excited about the future. After a couple of days of meetings, I landed back in Atlanta, energized about the doors God planned to open. I could feel Him working and was waiting for that sign. Well, that sign came when a recruiter from Microsoft reached out and talked to me about an intriguing opportunity: helping start up an inside sales organization within the company.

At that time, I wondered why Microsoft would launch a start-up within their already established company—I didn't believe such a market could exist. Well, it was true! I did four Skype interviews and prayed about having the opportunity to work at a Fortune 100 company. At the time, I had recently bought a home and was planting roots in Atlanta. Sometimes, when you happen to stumble on your path, you don't have to figure out which direction to travel. I knew I was going to move to Fargo and start a brand-new journey. And I did just that— in the middle of nowhere, I found out who I was! However, what I thought was a crazy decision turned out to be the best move I ever made in my professional career. That decision helped me grow as a person as well.

Now, let me help you visualize why moving to Fargo was my FIND. When I arrived in Fargo, I was low on cash and ready to relocate. I wanted to do what I needed to make it in a new space. Most people can't even locate Fargo on the map, but I always said Fargo, "like the movie", when I mentioned where I had moved. While in Fargo, I took an entry-level job at Microsoft Inside Sales. Did I think I was capable of more? Definitely. However, my desire to learn the business was more important than a title. One thing you learn from working for your family, or from growing up in that kind of environment is the value of knowing how to do everything concerning your business, or area of expertise. More importantly, you must have a strong desire to learn everything about your work. I applied that mindset to my new position at Microsoft.

During this time, everything was new, and my curiosity helped me accelerate my onboarding process with the company. Innately, I wanted to help, and lead my peers through incredibly ambiguous times. All I wanted to do was work hard to be the best representative on the team. Every day, I had opportunities to develop my work ethic, learn more about who I wanted to become, and work relentlessly to make that happen. I wanted to compete at a high level against some of the most intelligent people on the planet. I did that, and I did it well.

Let me tell you, sometimes you need to step back and look at your circumstances. When doing so, look at what is happening both to, and around you. What is causing the challenges or successes? How can you share that magic with others? I started in Fargo as a Sales Development Specialist (SDS). As an SDS, my role was to assess and qualify by ranking opportunities as highly likely to purchase and pass them to another team member to close. One thing I learned was that your real character shines when you're put in a situation of discomfort. Your ability to survive and exceed expectations is unmasked, and reality stares back at you as never before. Another lesson I learned was that I had an excellent opportunity to grow with the business, and that is what I did. I realized that I needed to take the time to meet people from both in and out of my reporting structure. In my corporate life, I like to focus a lot on relationships. That is reflected in my hustle, and more importantly, in my newfound swagger. The bottom line remains, however, and that is: don't focus on things (or relationships) that do not contribute in some way to your larger, lifetime goals.

While in Fargo, I learned that you could work extremely hard, and benefit from that effort time and time again. The ability to find what I enjoyed and then cultivate it with my overall goals in mind helped me to experience success early on. Continue to search for your "success engine". What is the right formula for you? I knew that mine was faith, focus, and a relentless pursuit of excellence. The major element there was and still is the unwavering faith that God would guide me along the way and help me to prioritize the order of my next steps. He will do the same for you! Trust in that process and let Him sculpt you as He deems necessary. To enable that level of trust, you have to let go of who *you* think you are and focus on who *God* wants you to become. Invest in being uncomfortable, as I was when I moved to Fargo.

Far removed from the distractions and noise, I was surrounded by peace, and I paused. That moment of stillness created control, which was something I had lost during my time in Atlanta. With control, you can accomplish anything within any amount of time. You must dilute divisive barriers and indulge yourself in positivity progress. Find prescriptive action points that trigger your success signals. Follow that beat, and you will listen in on the beautiful melody of your personal rhythm. Trust me: it sounds magical and motivational, and it is! It is the sound of your mind, body, and soul clicking together and letting your "most high" know you have reached awareness. I knew that once I became aware, I had attained personal power...A source of strength unleashed towards my constant and consistent efforts to be the best—similar to the way professional athletes, musicians, or moguls push towards continual happiness. That kind of drive and vision will propel you to engage in everything you enjoy, and love!

What I experienced in Fargo was the opportunity to step away from the usual grind and recharge my spirit. Recharging is about making an intentional commitment to yourself! It's about accepting how critical your personal success and progress is in terms of getting you to that next winning moment. When I looked at the 4F®™ Model and the FIND, my perspective went beyond finding what dreams I had. Those had been lost in the accident months before. I had to look deeper within myself; I had to find me again...the person who wanted to be truly successful. I did not want the façade, or the "front man" I created to hide behind in the past when things were not going well. Finding myself also became about discovering those inner gifts that I knew had existed my entire life.

Somehow, the focus became so narrowed on material gains and material satisfaction that I lost sight of what was important to my growth as a person. I needed to discover the essence of my presence in the world. It is very easy in this life to become tremendously invested in seeking the respect and attention of others or accumulating "likes" on social media; in the process, we go off course. In my own experiences, I lost that hustle and grind on which I prided my existence. The accident helped me realize that. Afterwards, I had the opportunity to be strict with myself, to refocus, and to stop blaming others for my decisions. It was time to rest up and then get back into the driver's seat of my destiny. It was time for me to commit and lock in. Are you locked in? If not, take time to recharge and find out who you are: identify your core capabilities. You know how to find your strengths when times are good, and you feel on top of the world, but what about when times are tough? Do you have the inner strength to withstand these vulnerable times, or is there someone else "recharging" you who could potentially remove your happiness, or success? How much is success and being great worth to you? Understand that each decision you make has positive and negative outcomes. The choices and the results go together! Recharge your personal mission to ensure that nothing can impede you from going full force and head-on into your next opportunity.

Spending time alone, reflecting on what is important to you, is the best thing you can do to prepare for greatness! Don't take for granted

how incredible you are, and that there is something inside you yearning to get out for the world
to see! Tap into the real you and see what comes
out. I promise it will be worth it! My first year in
Fargo, I was able to hit *refresh* on what I wanted
to display to the world. I had the opportunity to
be reborn, so to speak, and I realized that what I
had to show to the world was beautiful. I worked
at one of the top companies globally, and experienced amazing moments that would lead to some
powerful opportunities later in the journey. And
when I say, "powerful opportunities," I mean it!
The point is that no matter what you think about
an opportunity, give it time to find you as well. My
time as an entry-level salesperson was not about
my role at the time, but it was about humility and
my desire to learn a new business from the ground
up—to take control of my destiny and follow the
path to the goals I set out to reach.

Two and a half years ago, that goal was to move
to the Pacific Northwest and work at Microsoft
headquarters. I had fallen in love with the company that gave me a second chance to prove who

I was and what I was capable of becoming. What I saw in myself, Microsoft also saw in me. We found each other, and that has created a tremendous momentum, and a healthy relationship in which I invest and contribute 100 percent of myself every day. Don't worry, I am not asking you to give up on any entrepreneurial endeavor, or start-up project that's been brewing for a while. I am letting you know that I have that spirit embedded in my DNA, as you may well have too. I have taken an opportunity to share my talents within a global organization and with some of the most gifted people on the planet, and I could not be happier.

After my accident, my journey was not about where I came from, but what I wanted to do, and who I wanted to be moving forward. The time alone in Fargo had terrific benefits for me, including the opportunity to travel to Dublin, Ireland, continue building my relationship with my father, and spend time with my sister and her growing family that includes my two nieces. Often, we do not see the benefit of an opportunity until it's over. The positive impacts of moving to Fargo were immediate and was beautiful, as I re-evalu-ated personal interests, and reinvested in the fam-ily and friends who would help plug love back into my torn fibers. Always remember that a situation that does not liberate or stimulate your deepest desires is not something you want to spend your time on. I knew that the accident was a catalyst for me to reconsider my path and find what I was built to become. Finding that path is difficult, but as you will learn from the stories to come, I worked relentlessly to identify and protect what I discovered. I promise that it is worth investing in and seeing your full potential come to life.

The 4F®™ Model is not a perfect playbook or instruction manual to make your biggest dreams come to fruition. However, it can be a framework or compass to move you in the right direction, lev-eraged to position your mindset to create magic. No longer could I cloud my thinking and expect a tangible outcome. I had to recharge so I could go back into the world and not just compete but dom-inate. I was ready to go harder than ever toward a goal. Write those ideas and feelings down—it will work for you if you want it badly enough. No one can make you successful except you! Recharge and give yourself the infinite energy to be the best version of yourself. Spend time looking not at what is in right front of you but focus on finding what is beyond you. The FIND is the first step in this journey!

"Silence between the notes is what composes the music."

—Taylor Harps

COLLISION COURSE

August 16, 2016
Fargo, North Dakota

6

Blue Collar Grind

Momentum is defined as the impetus an object gains when in motion. Impetus is the force or energy with which a body moves. Momentum is important in overcoming life's challenges and utilizing the 4F®™ Model. To transform the four steps into massive, powerful breakthroughs, you need momentum. Without this energy and electricity running through my veins, I don't think my second year at Microsoft would have turned out the way it did. I had put my 2014 accident in the rearview, because I was tired of the burden of thinking back to the negative decisions, reactions, and opinions; I forgave myself for everything. At that very moment, I was able to stay locked in and focus on transformation. My momentum was so high that I moved into the next part of the model with full force. That next step is FOCUS.

Focus is about locking in on your success target with precision and accuracy and firing yourself through any obstacle that tries to impede your progress—anything that attempts to slow that momentum! When I was in Fargo, things started to click and at a high velocity. The training from my more formal education of commitment to the community, investing in others' success deliberately, and imagining my best self were all happening at the same time. This happened as I got promoted to an account manager in Microsoft's corporate customer segment. The anticipation of a new experience was thrilling, but I was afraid of the journey looming in the near distance. I worried about the critics thinking our team was too inexperienced, or the more senior folks imagining the possibility that the team may be in over our heads or matching our field counterparts' previous year's performance as the top area in the United States for our segment. Deep down in spirit, I was encouraged by the people and resources positioned to help us be successful.

When I received my accounts, I immediately went into entrepreneur mode. I had 168 accounts between Los Angeles and Greater Salt Lake City. Therefore, I had to lock in and get after the new business I was responsible for and figure out how to grow the territory. As I committed myself to the process, I realized that my previous experiences being in my stepfather's business, being around my mother as a consultant, and starting Burks & Bailey (Burks & Bailey was a bow tie company I cofounded a couple of years prior but was no longer operating) would emerge as extremely valuable moments in helping me to be successful. Instead of focusing on corporate protocol and processes that were extremely time-consuming, I decided to trust my instincts and just run the business. Fast forward to a year later, and I finished number one across the United States corporate space for inside sales. Let me tell you about the lessons learned along the way that helped me accomplish that success. It all started with FOCUS.

Although I was challenging my former self to become greater when I moved to Fargo, I did not anticipate becoming a good seller. I will take some credit, but there were a lot of people motivating me to be successful. Sometimes, others see something good (or great) in you long before you do. Sales often appeared to me as a sport: a game in which only those that were winning survived long enough to see the fruits of their labor. The task was long, hard, and difficult in that every day was a new opportunity to close the revenue gap while helping our customers achieve more with the technology. My focus was not to be a great seller, but a great advocate or voice for my customer to win with Microsoft. If the customer felt they were winning, I was surely going to win in the end if everything was done in great spirit. Selling is such a magical, yet unrelenting experience as you ebb and flow with the various buying journeys of your customers.

As the year pushed through, I realized that I was evolving into something more than a good seller. My experiences as an entrepreneur were unleashing themselves as I connected with partners, built an internal network, and increased my influence with customers. This was done by truly committing to be the best. I didn't know that I would finish at the top, but I was committed to do whatever it took to see my name in contention. A long time ago, I used to think I would be a top college prospect for basketball or tennis. The reality is that I was good, but I wasn't committed.

Back then, I enjoyed the competition, but not the sacrifice. Sometimes you need a reality check to realize that you have greatness stirring inside of you that wants to get out—that is God's blessing fighting to reach the surface for everyone to enjoy, and for those around you to benefit from your talent. I realized that my blessing was a renewed sense of gratitude. I was humbled by walking away from the car accident scratch free, and I knew it was time to thank Him again by giving everything I had to be successful in this phase of my life as a customer advocate. Whether it was long nights at the office or days filled with customer calls, I knew that every second I invested in being great would result in His favor.

Although I had a great year, I noticed something else along this part of my journey. I was so focused that I forgot to really and genuinely help others reach their ultimate potential. Often, you see that leaders are called, not chosen. I knew that with my success, I needed to learn how to help others. As you see yourself succeed, do not forget that people are watching you grind towards your greatness. No one ever becomes successful without the help from or sacrifices of other individuals willing to see them shine. During this time of perceived greatness, I adopted the "lone wolf" attitude, but I soon realized that not finding the right balance could be extremely detrimental to my professional and personal advancement. However, I do want to share a bit of insight I learned after reflecting on this period of my life. Being a lone wolf is not about being unwilling to play with others or the inability to commit to teamwork. In my experience, it was the exact opposite. This "loner" attribute is about leading by example and bringing the team to a positive destination—one filled with collective success and driven by the ability to go off and execute tasks strongly enough to propel the entire team. If you find yourself feeling like the lone wolf in your daily activities, embrace that feeling! Embrace the fact that you have leadership tendencies that need to be cultivated in order for you to achieve greatness. While pursuing your individual achievements, please do not forget to bring someone with you! That part of the journey is much sweeter when you help someone else experience victory too.

Continuing with that theme, being a lone wolf means you may have to surround yourself with others who are as willing to look greatness in the face as you are. I started to gravitate towards others who were masters at their craft, and I began watching successful people I admire consistently WIN! Through observation or conversation, and without restraint, I was able to lock in and focus on being a wolf. People not committed to success may not fully comprehend the next few sentences. Sometimes you must shed dead weight—get rid of people or things around you that are susceptible to becoming sheep who follow blindly. When I started this evolution to separate myself and commit to greatness, close friends stopped engaging, and I removed things that slowed me down from my routine. I reinvested in always making sure I put in place the critical components I personally needed. My advice to you is to pivot towards content or communities that create value, as opposed to catastrophe.

When I moved to Fargo, my friends and family thought I was a bit crazy. Honestly, I was getting a little concerned as well about my state of mind. In retrospect, that decision was the catalyst to the start of everything going on in my life today. I had close friends who thought I was mad, but still supported me every step of the journey. These friends are like-minded *wolves* too! Hard work pays off; it always pays off. When I decided to move to Fargo, I wrote down a goal along with a set of Bible scriptures on large poster paper. The goal was to complete two years in Fargo, and then experience life with Microsoft at the "mothership" in Redmond, Washington.

Redmond is the site of Microsoft headquarters, just outside of the greater Seattle area.

I was in a relationship at the time and remember telling my partner that I would be in Seattle within twenty-four months. Have you ever received a look of "Yeah, right..." in your life? Hers was this look full of doubt. I will say that when you are committed to something, you should not give anyone the power to deter you by asking them to see your vision. Go after that vision, and do not stop until you have it in your possession! The best and most rewarding feeling in the world is to commit to a goal, proceed to execute it at the highest levels, and ultimately, achieve it! However, I won't tell you that it was all good and rosy. Let me share the meaning of hard work...Do not ever think for a second that someone will give you anything just "because". If you do, life will be harder than it needs to be. What you need to focus on is investing every ounce of yourself into your destiny.

I didn't know I would be in Seattle in twenty-four months, but each day in Fargo, I gave everything I had (and more) to make it happen. If you do not work harder and smarter than others around you, success will always be an arm's-length reach away. Don't sell yourself short by doing fifty percent, or ninety-nine percent of the effort! Go for the full one hundred percent and then some, if you have it in you. My mother always told me that "you will only get out what you put in," and this was the time in my life that I proved her right. Prove yourself right by giving it your all! It will be worth it when the victory comes, and you accomplish your goals. As I mentioned earlier, I gave up a lot of fun nights and relaxation to practice my craft. I learned something new about my customers each day that I could leverage or infuse into our business transformation conversations. You have to act the same way when working towards your dreams! Learn something every day that helps you get one inch closer to victory.

You are probably asking, "Well, did it work for you?" Simply put, yes! I didn't move to Seattle in twenty-four months, but I had an accepted offer signed in May 2017. That was twenty-two months ahead of schedule, and a direct result of hard work! Trust me, hard work pays off—it always does!

"You have to
be odd to be
number one."

—Carlton Curry II

COLLISION COURSE

July 24, 2017
Seattle, Washington

7

Stay L.I.T.

At this point in my journey, the 4F®™ Model pushed me towards feeding my momentum. The third step in the model is all about feeding or investing more into the current moment. Lock into your present success while preparing for the next level of greatness. Before that can come to fruition, you must think about how to "Stay L.I.T." This concept does not imply just being confident or cool, as the popular songs may put it today. My referencing of the term is about humility, deference, and general gratitude for every element of success you experience on your journey. This is about the ability to stay *Living in Triumph* (or L.I.T.) each step of the way. Living in Triumph is about consciously maintaining who you are, while accomplishing what you hope to become in the future. Sometimes, it is as simple as riding your own wave and hoping you can last long enough to get to the other side. There will be times when you have to embrace being in your glory!

Before moving to Seattle, I was selected to present a demo at the all-company conference in

Las Vegas. This is a weeklong celebration during which all the business folks from around the organization praise the great work of others, while leadership points the ship in the desired direction for the upcoming fiscal year. This event was such a grand opportunity and excellent example of staying L.I.T. The chance was really like a corporate bucket list item if you worked at Microsoft, in that I would be giving a demo as part of a senior executive's main stage presentation. This was a defining moment for me in which I could genuinely celebrate my success and share the great work of countless others in front of the entire company (in person and streaming). After giving the demo, there were numerous emails, text messages, phone calls, and handshakes praising my efforts. I was just honored to be able to do something of that scale that early in my career. It provided so much self-confidence that would flow over into other experiences in my current role. I wanted to share this story because it was the crucial moment of a long journey. I was able to stand in front of my peers as a new man after two years of self-discovery and relentless hard work. There was no second-guessing my abilities or talent at this point. Experienced firsthand, that moment was sheer triumph defined by a twelve-minute presentation. All the hours, tears, and sacrifice paid off in that instant. Think about your defining moment, or what it might be, and whether you are preparing yourself for glory. Step outside of your current tribulation to see what God may have in store as you consider your next move. I didn't know this opportunity would come, but I was damn sure I was going to be ready when it did. Will you be ready?

The other valuable lesson I learned from staying L.I.T. was about embracing your authentic self. Nothing will happen if you are constantly envious of others, or not true to yourself. Before I moved to Fargo, I was living a life that was not my own. I was not yet a CEO, but operated as one in a negative way, which didn't help me grow. Despite my talents or abilities, that was a static mindset no matter what my subconscious was telling me. The person I was then was afraid of his own dreams! The day of the accident helped me realize that it was time to stop dreaming, and start acting to make these dreams come alive. This started with proactively ensuring I was enjoying life and having fun. If you follow me on Instagram (@catchpt), you will notice that images of the world fill the screen. My whole philosophy behind choosing this social handle was that instead of dreaming about that life, I decided to go out and *catch* it! You should do the same! Forget waiting for something to happen and go take it! Make the next move and take the risk to receive the reward. The worst thing that can happen is that you do nothing, and wonder what could've happened if you had made that leap. Stop being afraid of the possibilities and confront them with confidence! Life is way too short to second-guess yourself, and this is not a dress rehearsal. You are on prime time every day of your life! Take that as a challenge, and stay L.I.T.

Now that I am in Seattle, each day is sweet because I know the grind to get here was so tough. The journey was daunting and sometimes lonely, but I made it through. You will also make it through! Each of us will encounter many mountains that seem too high, but we scale them anyway. I climbed a few mountains, and when I finished those, I searched for a bigger one. Do it! Challenge yourself to ride your wave of greatness for as long as you can. What counts is the ride, and that we lock in for as long as is necessary to reach our goals. My successes have come with sacrifices, and yours will not be any different. However, the best things in life come with sacrifice, so get ready for it! I moved two time zones away from home, alone, to fulfill my dreams, and I am still going! Through taking those leaps of faith, I was able to accomplish a goal I had set three years before, and I am now setting new ones. I want more and will have more because I am committed to making it happen.

Aside from my experiences, I have seen my close friends achieve so much more from their lives by taking risks too. Whether it was quitting their corporate jobs to pursue real estate, launching a fedora brand, growing an interior design business, or sculpting bodies through fitness, my friends have identified their blessings and pushed towards them without fear. This commitment is defined by the sheer willingness to attempt. We pride ourselves within our group as doers, and leaders; we want to inspire others who are losing out by waiting for someone else to do it first. That is what motivated me to share this story with you in the first place! Watching and being able to experience my closest friends exemplify how they stay L.I.T. has driven me to express what I can share. Triumph is about taking control of this one life, and making each second mean something to yourself, and the world! It is about colliding with your own hopes and dreams and becoming everything God intended you to be—a perfectly imperfect reflection of his (or her) own being.

To achieve this, don't be afraid to chase what scares you. Facing your fears that will make you great and help you to achieve success! *Collision Course* is about transforming our challenges in life into massively powerful breakthroughs that propel us to achieve more than we could imagine.

These challenges are the mountains we must climb in order to reach the top and see what lies beyond. The climb will never be easy or straightforward, so don't expect that! However, it will be filled with small wins that keep you motivated to reach the peak. When you do reach that mountaintop, revel in your success and enjoy what you have accomplished. Always celebrate what you do! The challenge you may have is shedding that success and preparing for something tougher...a more complicated problem pushing you to the edge of what you know about yourself today.

A long time ago, I came up with the phrase, "Each Accomplishment Remembers Nothing" (or EARN) to keep inspiring and motivating me to go after more. Time is finite, and the most precious resource known to humanity. What you do with it matters! But don't lose sight of the fact that while you are celebrating the wins, someone is learning from their losses. Get and stay L.I.T. as you accelerate to your massive, and powerful breakthroughs!

"The Best
Never Rest."

—Jeremy Shipp

COLLISION COURSE

June 11, 2018

Home

8

Unwritten

If you made it this far in the book, it means that you are serious about pursuing your purpose. The reality is of what I am expressing is a simple testimony to help others experience what I have been for the last few years – my purpose. Growing up I really wanted to be a professional athlete, but through life's experiences I learned that I could go "pro" in my purpose. That is powerful to experience! Manifesting what you were placed on the earth to become is about living enough to have losses and lessons that you can learn from over time.

The reality is that no one that is successful and with a story to tell didn't experience tough times or moments filled with doubt. That doubt is fear and your success want you to embrace it, so you can experience abundance. Where I am at today is not my final destination on this journey. Pursuing your purpose is a life-long commitment. Purpose will enable you to understand your greatness. However, you must realize that achieving greatness is a continuous process. It is an infinite loop playing on *repeat* throughout our lives. Over and over, we will be challenged and placed in predicaments that push our human limitations emotionally, mentally, physically, etc., until we either break, or experience a breakthrough.

During that process, the 4F®™ Model will help you stay on course and come through victorious on the other side. Each of those breakthroughs are FACTS – the last step of the 4F®™ Model. Facts are the outcomes or victories experienced along the way. The small wins that you mark as tallies on the scoreboard but may not celebrate as much. I challenge you to celebrate each accomplishment. Analyze the activities and actions that went into achieving that success, because it will help you as you elevate into your next level.

The interesting component of the 4F®™ Model is the facts. Without them, how will you know if you did anything successful? Facts are the telemetry required to gauge where improvements can be achieved or how to refine an element that is working well. Keep an inventory of these facts, because you never know when you will need them along the journey. Build on your accomplishments and never stop winning. Winning is more than getting the sought after "W" or moment to tout your success – it is about accepting your purpose bestowed upon you by your creator to live in his view of what you should be in this life. Take that responsibility seriously as many people strive each day to reach a place of purpose or fulfillment. Hold on to that feeling!

In addition, create that feeling for others that are looking at you to lead them along the journey. The tide or your "wave" should rise all ships and not just your own. Build a legacy that echoes into eternity as each fact is chiseled mark in your story. What do you want it to say? When I finished the 4F®™ Model in theory, my challenge became to implement the methodology into real-life. A challenge focused on going through the daily activities to reach my success. The toughest area in my life was figuring out to achieve balance. Balance is extremely elusive in a world filled with missed text messages, social media posts, career pursuits, relationships, and everything else. I knew that to even write this book would require a commitment to discovering balance. How did I do it? The reality is that you must learn to say "no" to areas or things in your ethos not providing positive returns. Just like stocks and knowing when to buy or sell. You must be clear on what can positively influence the desired outcomes you want for your life.

The most important lesson I can share is to value your time. Balance is achieved through placing a price on what you can invest yourself into in each situation. This requires the ability to evaluate worth – whether in people, projects, business deals, relationships, etc. – you must know your worth! As I was writing this last piece of the book, I wanted to ensure my readers understood that I eliminated any distractions that did not help me complete this story. I valued my time and my dreams! Don't let anything (or anyone) devalue your worth by taking you away from your purpose. Stay focused on the execution, so you can get the facts. You need these to tell your story of transforming life's challenges into powerful break-throughs. I know it is hard to finish a story that is not yet over, so realize the best is yet to come. The manuscript of your life is partly complete, and you have plenty of time to write whatever you want for the future lines. The life you want is not about what is in front of you—what is beyond matters the most, and those are the facts! I cannot wait to see what you become...

"Life is not what lies in front of you. It's what is beyond you that really matters."

—Phil Terrill

What is your purpose? (FIND)

Write them down! Commitment starts with copying ideas from your mind and putting them on paper!

_____

_____

_____

_____

_____

_____

_____

_____

_____

_____

_____

_____

How will you reach or fulfill your purpose? (FOCUS)

Are there distractions or limitations that exist for you today that could impede the momentum you seek?

_____

_____

_____

_____

_____

_____

_____

_____

_____

_____

_____

_____

What will ensure you are successful and committed to victory? (FEED)

Think about what you need to accomplish the goal. Do you require resources, people, or experiences to get you there?

_____

_____

_____

_____

_____

_____

_____

_____

_____

_____

_____

_____

_____

What results are being generated from your actions? (FACTS)

The results you create will be helpful when reflecting about the journey later! Have you made the progress you were hoping to make?

_____

_____

_____

_____

_____

_____

_____

_____

_____

_____

_____

_____

_____

Dedication & Acknowledgements

This book is dedicated to the visionaries, entrepreneurs, dreamers, hustlers, grinders, 9-to-5ers, and the next generation of innovators yet to come. *Collision Course* is a guide to help you effectively break down barriers and continue to achieve your greatness. *Collision Course* focuses on your gifts and abilities by continually analyzing opportunities and delivering results that transcend your current perspective. You have incredible talents and blessings—let them shine in everything you do!

To my siblings and closest friends, the greatest ability to passionately write *Collison Course* and successfully implement the 4F®™ model in my life has been based on the unconditional support of the team around me who don't quit, don't stop, and love strong. They inspire, influence, engage, and support me, and I believe that is the greatest blessing any person can have—a life filled with love and support from close friends. Trust me: it makes it all so much easier, and so worth it!

To my parents, thank you for your support, love, and lessons. A child learns so much from what his or her parents say, and the environments they enable you to be in, but I have gained so much more than the perks of their hard work. I have learned from who you are, and what you do. The genuine acts of parenthood and the positive influence you have been in my life and the lives of others are invaluable blessings that nothing can replace. Keep striving and leading our family!

To my readers, I believe in the abilities and commitment you possess to be incredible! Do not stop pushing or remembering that you are amazing. You have achieved and will continue to make monumental impacts that influence the global direction of our society. Keep thinking! Keep grinding! Keep challenging! Keep growing! Now is the time to prepare for the life you imagine for tomorrow!

I love everyone and thank you for your support!

About the Author

Phil Terrill is a builder! From building consumer brands to world-class, sales organizations, he is right at the heart of sharing experiences that are worth their weight. With his passion for empowering people, it is no surprise that *Collision Course* would be the platform to convey those stories. As an entrepreneur, philanthropist, and global leader, Phil is constantly striving to encourage his community to pour into their purpose. Phil is committed to building the lives of others by sharing his testimony about an experience that truly changed the trajectory of his life. The transparency and truth in his writing will be the foundation of success for anyone.

Today, Phil is a Global Program Manager at Microsoft. Prior to Microsoft, Phil worked for The Burks Companies in Atlanta (GA) helping a family enterprise deliver facilities management solutions across the Southeast. He also spent time working with MillerCoors, formerly Miller Brewing Company, in downtown Chicago (IL). Phil received his B.S. in Marketing from Tuskegee University.

Phil resides in St. Paul, Minnesota and enjoys traveling the world, learning about new cultures, spending time with family, and living life to the fullest.

You can learn more about Phil's journey at: www .readcollisioncourse.com.

CPSIA information can be obtained
at www.ICGtesting.com
Printed in the USA
LVHW011612210119
604682LV00015B/216/P

9 781543 935691